HATCHLING

Selected Poems

Laura Jo Maschal

© Copyright 2014 by Laura Jo Maschal
All rights reserved.

Published by Hatchling Press
HatchlingPress.com
United States of America

Cover Art by Sara Cancian
Cover Design by Eric Bourgeois

ISBN-13: 978-0692218709
ISBN-10: 069221870X

For Nature & Spirit

With gratitude to...

Peter. For never once complaining.

Mia. For listening, though none of these poems is about math.

Emma. For all the encouragement.

Jeanne. For her brilliant insights and skillful edits.

The LBI Writers Group. For calling me a writer.

The community. For all the people, places, critters, ancestors and seasons that brought me here.

You, reader. For sharing the journey.

Contents

The Grasshopper	9
The Purple Martin House	10
Autumn Breath	12
Hatchling	13
Two Words	14
Meteor	16
Kingdom Done	17
Riptide	18
Empty Shells	19
Legacy	20
Cancer	21
I Hold You In My Teeth	22
Our Dream Drive Off a Cliff	24
My Father's Fists	25
Seedling	26
Psychometry and Fireflies	28
Returning Home: A Dog's Blessing	29

Bee	30
The Gardener	32
You Leave	33
Grandmother Spider	34
Seeing a Praying Mantis Always Feels Like a Good Omen	35
P.syringae	36
Weekend Tribal Council	37
Swords of Light	38
Silent Spring	39
More Nerve Than Heart	40
Endless Breath	42
Sweet Bird of Disaster	43
What Do You Dream Of?	44
Winter Prayer	46
Betwixt and Between	47
Index of First Lines	48

The Grasshopper ☙

You wanted a sense of sacredness to rise up,
as you lay stretched out
on your belly, legs bent skyward,

like that pale grasshopper,
flaring like a lit match
from the sun-bleached stones,

a great cacophony of flapping,
bigger than its whole body,
bigger than its skittering giant leap.

The grasshopper never asks permission
or whether it is worthy of the world.
Enough. I am. Enough. It rasps on tinder legs.

You wanted the fire of recognition,
of being known by something spirited and wild,
proof of your sacred, untamable nature,

eye to eye with that grasshopper; heart,
pressed against a hot, hard sea of pebbles,
beating like a paper wing.

The Purple Martin House ❦

The purple martin house blew over,
chicks and all; that particular gust
a wrecking ball against its sturdy metal post.
It lay on the dock like the broken bones
of some ancient creature,
shown up in flashes of white,
jagged angles against the black storm.

Like the unguarded thoughts of a madman,
birds flew off in every direction,
only to return again and again
throughout the night. Hovering
and lifting, they beat time against the
spin of the earth, flying toward
a dawn some 93 million miles distant.

In the morning, we moved softly
among the murmurings,
the day filled with blue and the smells
of water and grass, seaweed and honeysuckle.
We pieced together splintered fragments,
lifted the house high enough for the weary
skittering feet of the suspended flock
to find purchase, huddled babes, at last.

In the sedge pool, close on,
bobbed the broken and iridescent body
of a single martin, an adult female,
dark against the milky green of the settling bay.
I thought of her brave trial over the course
of the fatal night and realized:
it isn't the spirit of the dead that haunts us,
but rather, our own spirit waking, finally, to life.

Autumn Breath ☙

You could be anywhere really,
on an Autumn day,
when the smell of wood smoke –
even just the hint of it –
opens all your hidden passages.

It rises like a new faith, a warm sun
and you breathe deeply
into its promise.

If you happen to look,
up and down the
hushed woodland corridors,
fevered trees are
tossing off their lung bodies.

Bold exhalations of red and gold and ash
settle like an ancient devotion.
A prayer for old tree bones.

You imagine how these trees
hold the fires of the sun,
close and still in their dark veins –
mapping a solar journey, ring upon ring,
all through the breathless winter.

Hatchling ☙

Some poems nest
within themselves
a particular phrase,
an aching and tenuous
combination of words
that speak to the spirit,
like a small bird
unfolding itself.

Other times,
a poem can be filled
with the simplicity
of ordinary words,
yet still weave together
an idea of astonishing loveliness,
bound and delicate.
Whole as a small blue egg.

Such exquisite pain,
those first flutterings
as the heart cracks open.

Two Words ⚘

That text
could've been any two words,
after so much time had passed
without one.

For instance,
I'm sorry
or
Miss you

would have grown Jack's own
beanstalk bridge between us,
thick and lush as jungle vines.

Even
I'm broke
or
Fuck you

could have sparked my dormant ire –
your warning shot
fired across my bow.

Or *please*,
some absurd musing to pique or confuse,
like a dubbed Bruce Lee movie
with French subtitles.

Tofu bacon
or
Nice bindi!

But it wasn't.
And those two words glowed dully –
electronic embers, suspended,
in cold black space:

She's dead.

Meteor ☙

I read in the newspaper once
about a meteor shower:
Flaming balls of light
raining down,
like spring hailstones
on the prairie.
So many in a single minute,
all those fiery streaks stood still
as the earth sped by.

And the people who saw?
They flung themselves
to the ground, clutching
fistfuls of dirt,
pressing dampened cheeks
into the empty fields
of their farmlands,
so dizzied were they
by their own awareness.

The newspaper called it madness.

Kingdom Done ☙

I startled up a hive of thick black ants;
a hidden bastion beside the garden shed.
Pottery turrets toppled,
loam catacombs collapsed.

How the buxom matrons moved!
Frantic to guard their cache: eggs
laid out in neat rows, milky white,
wriggling with larval jelly.

Revulsion rose up in me –
righteous unholy crusader. I brandished
the garden hose like a weapon,
sent the ant fortress swirling into a ditch.

In the muddy aftermath, a pale green spider –
cursed barbarian – dropped from a leaf
and plucked the last egg, mired,
still trembling, from the ruins.

How the battle lines blurred
between the natural and the sacred
as I wept for our vanished kingdoms,
for all our ravaged remains.

Riptide ☙

I think about how you saved me
by accident that September
morning on the empty shore.

How the sleepy water suddenly
awoke; hungrily pulled me to it.
How I clutched your upraised hand.

Your face smiling, then startled
as my frantic, churning feet
found your thigh, shoved mightily.

I never even looked back.

Later we ate a picnic lunch
on the hot sand and I whispered,
"I could've drowned."

"But you didn't," you grinned, mouth
full of peanut butter sandwich.
We never spoke of it again.

Sometimes, lying awake, I pull that day out,
hold it in the dark – smooth and heavy as a river rock –
and lament its lack of jagged edges.

Empty Shells ತಾ

It wasn't malice, no, not malice
that sent my fingers dipping into nature's bucket.
I pulled up scallop after scallop, wedged
a lethal fingernail into each
weighty, spitting, corrugated fist.

I splayed the singular trembling muscle inside.
Was it a heart? A foot?
"Which of these will save you?" I challenged
again and again, until my nails were dull,
soggy as their exposed mollusk bellies.

The sea had her own questions
as she slipped in and split our houses,
once so tightly held, wide open.
I tremble with the not knowing
for fear she asks again. And again.

I see those empty shells now, each
grayed and floppy as an old tin roof,
and think: *This was once somebody's home,
bound together by sinew and muscle and heart -*
and cradle it against my own.

And the scallop gods keep whispering:
"See? See how we come unhinged?"

Legacy ☙

I want my life to mean something.
But really what I mean is:
I want some piece of me to carry on
beyond the limits of bone and bacteria;
a star fragment still shining
long after the body dies.

But what lost city ever held anything
but the temporary vainglories of
rubble and ash, roads and religion?

Meanwhile, the stars themselves
shine just as brightly, and I
run to the overgrown fields,
the layered canyons,
the black and boundless ocean,
where I can lean into their light.

Cancer ☙

You just keep thinking
of that one thing –
that One. Bad. Thing.

Oh how an undulating
shadow can maroon you
from the whole ocean

or a burn hole
can unravel a sea
of antique lace.

And yet, even as
the mind spirals
toward that dark flame,

you feel a hidden self
unfolding, shedding
your old life –

some stiff and broken
carapace that can
no longer hold you.

I Hold You In My Teeth ☙

I hold you in my teeth
nestled in the
fissures and grooves
of a permanent
molar landscape.

"There are small cracks," the dentist says.

All that life
with both of us in it,
bound in a mercurial cache
of you and me,
pulled from its orbit.

"It has to come out." he says.

As the drill bites down,
memories like fine dust
fly around my head
with the chips and shards
of silver.

"Just don't swallow," he says.

I ruminate on the grit,
that strange amalgam
of origins, extracted;
spit you out in a toxic swirl
of blackened bits.

"All your childhood fillings are gone," he says.

And my cursed,
inquisitive tongue
probes that cosmic hole.

Our Dream Drive Off a Cliff ☙

I would know this dream-place
if we ever visit again.

The mountainside awash in gold
as the road curves away.
How we skid and plummet
over the precipice.

In our fall, the screams of
recrimination tear away
with our lips; leaving us wordless,
smiling into the silence.

Our wild eyes, desperate
for what might have been,
plucked out in the face of
wonder at what is.

O, what beauty!

I reach for you even as the
delicate skin of memories
strips to gray matter
and breath.

Laid bare, sharp as bones,
in that final guttering respiration?

Love.

My Father's Fists ❧

He slams his fists.
For emphasis.

"MY FATHER WAS A SONOFABITCH –
ALIVE OR DEAD I DON'T CARE WHICH!"

Each un-spared rod can build a cage,
can grow a man from boy to rage.

Not the lashing of a leather strap,
but what of the child a tongue can trap?

Tiptoe through an eggshell meal
where a glass of milk can make you feel

pitifully small and very VERY BAD
because he's sooooo, oh so mad

that all his hate comes spilling out
like that milk, in a rush of angry shouts.

To get invisible, be the hare.
Find the gap. Stay there.

Frozen under shattered glass.
At once examined. At once looked past.

Unseen. Disconnect.
Focus on a tiny speck:

The thumbnail of a child's fist,
tightly curled, for emphasis.

Seedling ଔ

When I was a girl,
a seedling grew up
from a walnut
in our backyard.

I forgot it was hidden
in the tall summer grass
as I pushed the mower
ahead of me.

Senses drowned
in cutting smells,
metallic vibrations
roared through me.

Again and again,
I mowed
the fragile thing
down.

A ragged brown stick
poked up
in the wake of
my grass-stained haste.

Its will to live, to thrive
raced on, pulled
the tender seedling
to new heights —

even if just a breath
over the grasslings.
Slender stem? Woodier!
Foliage? More lush!

Until, finally, the dulled
mower blades of autumn
gave way.
The sturdy sapling prevailed.

I think of that seedling –
a tree now,
flourishing, determined;
its broad leafy canopy

throwing shadows
over both of us
every time
you cut me down.

Psychometry and Fireflies ☙

This book was loved before; carries a caress on its binding.
Fragile pages spark a resonance in my hands –
a ghost image of flickering, living light – bright as fireflies.

Emilie, October 9, 1941, carefully inscribed.
She is folded within these sheets, tucked between the night –
crisp with winesap and muskmelon – and the brink of war.

Emilie's heart flutters and lifts with its verses
while darkness huddles against her pale bedside lamp
and the moon floats above the bricks and mortar of a noisy city.

I turn the page with a hopeful hand.
What spark – bound in black, yellowed and brittle –
like the light of stars across time, will illumine *this* night?

Returning Home: A Dog's Blessing ☙

You curl beside me and I breathe you in –
like a mother checking her newborn
for fingers, toes, wholeness.

I breathe in the rich flavors of your fur,
cedar and earth,
the warm smell of popcorn paws.

I watch your belly rise and fall,
the envy of Yogis everywhere.

Each inhale slower and deeper than the last
until your seeing me
and dreaming me melt together.

In one long shuddering release,
you breathe me out –
with all your fears of our parting.

Bee ☙

Behold! The bee.
A swollen bullet
of honey and venom
on an erratic path
to Eden.

God's woofer
wrapped in sunlight and shadow,
blaring earth's hum,
a tiny speaker
on Nature's stereo.

Do you know me bee?

I want to squeeze your
velvety abdomen, spill
through your pencil point barb
all the sweetness and bitter of life
in inky strands of DNA.

Let me gather your essence
in powdery pollen bits,
then dance that hum
with certainty and abandon
across the page.

Do you know me bee?

I want to swallow you down.
Let your grace fill me up,
feel your stinger pierce me through
until pinpoints of pure light
shoot out through my skin.

The lost sister of the Pleiades – found.

The Gardener ☙

In the dark loam

of the garden,

I visit with ancestors.

Here, let me

comb out your bones,

resurrect you

in daffodils.

You Leave ∽

I need to breathe the trees

That particular elixir

Birch elm maple

Give what they are able

For me

For you

I pine

Grandmother Spider ❧

I sit in stillness,
barely breathe.
Mesmerized,
I watch you weave.

You've spun a world
upon your web
and woven me
into its thread.

Fragile strands
of silver lace
connect us with
uncommon grace.

With pen and heart,
in words so few,
I hope that I
can weave you too.

Seeing a Praying Mantis Always Feels Like a Good Omen ☙

Is it because they
seem so rare?
Like badass crickets
in Ninja-wear!

Is it the tilting head,
the crazy eyes?
Better not kill 'em
no matter their size.

Maybe seeing one
is a call to prayer.
To remind us
god is everywhere.

Whatever the reason,
I'm always surprised.
I bow to their antics,
most humbly advise:

"Pray little mantis.
And eat some flies."

P. syringae ଔ

Jack Frost microbes everywhere,
grow the rain out of thin air.

Sterile clouds are merely vapor,
dust and ash without a Shaper.

Rainmaker, snowfaller, hexagonal Creator.
Water dropper, steam riser, ice nucleator.

The clouds are alive, creating weather,
holding us and the atmosphere together.

Could science control these divining rods
or have we angered them enough, these gods?

Weekend Tribal Council ଓ

We came for different reasons –
Our roots as varied
as the roads that led us here.

The rain in the night beat the drum drum drum,
daring us to shout our ancestor prayers
as bold as bare branches. Reach!

"To create something wild and good," she said.
Each of us, flinging our voices,
like dry kindling,

to spark a fire in our minds.
And in the gray ashes of the dawn –
Look! Tiny buds are forming.

Swords of Light ☙

Sometimes I think about dying
as a reprieve from this habitual life,

a cosmic molecular firework,
a rearrangement of my starbody

into sleeker skin, looser fur.
Then the sun turns my head

with swords of light
piercing a dark and silent wood;

with pinkly glowing edges
of twilight on water;

with the sacred hum of leaves
lifted on a tremble of air;

and I am willful
as a child at bedtime,

tireless, begging for just
one minute more.

Silent Spring ☙

Our voices carry,
timbre travelling
along the roving branches
of satellites

as rooted cell towers
bear the fruit of our lives,
through bits and pixels
photo-synthesizing.

We gather kilobytes
against data plans
like nuts squirreled
in a wintry hollow.

And as our chatter
expands like kudzu
over the vast
canopy of coverage,

the tree in the yard
stands mute.

More Nerve Than Heart ☙

I am much less
broken heart
than severed nerve
when we fight
this way.

Heart damage can be fatal,
but a nerve!
Slice a nerve in two
and it will continue
to grow.

Nerves don't ask "Why?"
Or "Why bother?" Nerves just want
to be whole. This, I suppose,
is the nature of all living things –
this desire to be whole.

Laboriously, we grope
through the damaged tissue
of hurtful words and misdeeds,
your axon to my nucleus,
that we might reconnect.

Suddenly a mess of
hurry-up things
must happen, in order
to repair
that severed slice.

And they do. And it does!
Miraculously,
we heal.
But still, there is
this phantom pain.

Endless Breath ෬

See how the stars fall into you,
tell the same stories
our ancestors sang
around the fire.

How else to ask
the sky-questions that fill us?
Perhaps their long ago
chants rose up and up,

sparks suspended
on their breath,
only just now returning
home to you.

And as you fill the night
with your own sky-questions,
listen. Listen to the fire.
It sings in you.

Sweet Bird of Disaster ☙

Disaster shoves you from the nest
without a coat, and slams the door.

Control and permanence,
that sense of entitlement
wrapped up in bits and baubles –
all as ephemeral, as futile
as drifting, downy feathers
after the fox.

Now you are nose up to the window,
seeing for the first time
beyond the reflected world,
beyond the clutter of notions,
to your own true nature:
delicate and determined as a wing.

 Why, then, do you fly at the glass
and weep at its shattering?

What Do You Dream Of? ଓ

When I met the medicine man,
I dreamed of the rough, woolly
buffalo spirit and his hoof-beat drum.
I dreamed of wood smoke and cedar,
the rock people, those ancient ones before time,
before religion.

When I listen to the Tibetan singing bowls,
I dream of the sound trees make,
walking around in their forest kitchens –
and mists rising on the morning air,
and goats perched high on a mountainside.
Why goats? Why not goats?

What dreams run in your blood, or pool in the
deep well of your wild and dreaming mind?

I have dreamed of becoming a house,
her sashes thrown open to the sea,
filmy curtains flying wild in the purple twilight.
And of being hunched and held inside an egg,
the world a watery haze of capillary trees;
my body jarred from sleep, at the wonder of being born.

When I sit with dragonflies, their black needles
stitched neatly onto marsh threads,
I dream God is the wizard next door
and I am his apprentice.
In the morning he hands me the Galaxy,
swirling slowly in a broken teacup.

What dreams have you given your life to,
that they might spill over into the dark places?

Winter Prayer ○₃

I call upon the spirit of bear.
Let me hibernate in my dreams!
Enough running 'round in circles,
fat on the calories of honey, honey, honey.
Give me the spirit-food of introspection,
the sustenance of stillness.

Hurl me into that inky space
Between the borealis and
the lobes of my chattering brain.
Cradle me into the long winter's nap –
A quiet mind, some senseless void
where I can hear my own heart.

Let me be like the winter trees: stripped bare
of garish distractions, the roar of fluttering.
Fall away and leave me, while the sap runs slow.
Give me the tenacity of roots, silently
creeping into the earth, nourished
by darkness and the dirt of origins.

Betwixt and Between ❧

Oh sweet magic of the night!
When our minds are thick
with the sap of dreams
and what seems madness
under the hard-bitten
glare of sun suddenly fills us
with the heady fragrance of Truth
bursting into bloom
among the thorny defenses
of our withered longings.
Betwixt and between
that dream sigh of sleep
and the in-breath of waking,
we are green,
impassioned and impetuous.
Bold as lemons, ardent,
believing in our own god-ness again.

Index of First Lines

Behold! The bee.	30
Disaster shoves you from the nest	43
He slams his fists	25
I am much less	40
I call upon the spirit of bear.	46
I hold you in my teeth	22
I need to breathe the trees	33
I read in the newspaper once	16
I sit in stillness,	34
I startled up a hive of thick black ants;	17
I think about how you saved me	18
I want my life to mean something.	20
I would know this dream-place	24
In the dark loam	32
Is it because they	35
It wasn't malice, no, not malice	19
Jack Frost microbes everywhere,	36
Oh sweet magic of the night!	47
Our voices carry,	39
See how the stars fall into you,	42
Some poems nest	13
Sometimes I think about dying	38
That text	14
The purple martin house blew over,	10
This book was loved before...	28
We came for different reasons –	37
When I was a girl,	26
When I met the medicine man,	44
You could be anywhere really,	12
You curl beside me and I breathe you in –	29
You just keep thinking	21
You wanted a sense of sacredness to rise up,	9

www.ingramcontent.com/pod-product-compliance
Lightning Source LLC
Chambersburg PA
CBHW032104040426
42449CB00007B/1175